SPARROW ENVY

SPARROW ENVY

FIELD GUIDE TO BIRDS AND LESSER BEASTS

J. DREW LANHAM

HUB CITY PRESS
SPARTANBURG, SC

Cover Illustration: © Tristan Kronopawiro
Proofreaders: Kendall Owens, Betsy Teter
Editor: John Lane
Printed in Chelsea, Michigan by Sheridan Books

An earlier, prose version of "9 Rules For the Black Birder" appeared in *Orion*,
Nov./Dec. 2013, orionmagazine.org.

A shortened version of this book was first printed in 2016 by Holocene
Publishing in Spartanburg, South Carolina.

Library of Congress Cataloging-in-Publication Data
Names: Lanham, Drew, author.
Title: Sparrow Envy: A Field Guide to Birds and Lesser Beasts : poems
J. Drew Lanham.
Description: Spartanburg, SC : Hub City Press, 2021.
Identifiers:
  LCCN 2020047490
  ISBN 9781938235-81-8 (hardback)
  ISBN 9781938235-82-5 (ebook)
Subjects: LCGFT: Poetry.
Classification: LCC PS3614.O23 C58 2021 | DDC 813/.6—dc23
LC record available at https://lccn.loc.gov/2020047490 (edited)

Manufactured in the United States of America

HUB CITY PRESS
200 Ezell Street
Spartanburg, SC 29306
864.577.9349 | www.hubcity.org

To Martha, Incas, and Booming Ben—last of their kind passenger pigeon, Carolina parakeet and heath hen—and for all the other unnamed birds and beasts forever gone on through extinction's hellish door. These words of adoration, wonder, angst and joy are for those wild creatures yet remaining. Hold on. Hold on.

CONTENTS

BIRDS

LESSER BEASTS

MEANINGS & REGULATORY RAMBLE

BIRDS

CONSIDERING BIRDS

A heron waits at the water's edge—wondering.
Wade or wait—fish or not?
No multitudes to satisfy—no flock to feed.
Just one lone long-legged-longing thing.
Choose wisely wader,
wish and want won't will the hunger away.

Had I wings to fly how far would I wander? How high?
It is tasked to earthbound souls like mine
to worry over flight—
or falling.
A sparrow sings the knowing
a feather's lift is faith enough.

FIELD MARK 3: WOOD THRUSH ID (MADE SIMPLE)

It's not so much about identifying *what* birds are, as feeling *who* birds are. Head nods, jaw drops, smiles, tears and abject adoration, are all "feel marks" for identifying the wood thrush—a brown-backed, forest-singing soul seldom seen, but more often heard and felt deeply. As this bird pumped its heart out in auto three-part harmony, the one inside my own chest stopped beating for a while.

ON TIMBERDOODLE TIME

Yesterday, on twilight's descent to dark—a chord of woodcocks spiraled upward through descending night. Venus winked—called the stars out one by one. The wall-eyed birds fell back to earth "peenting" and twittering all the way down. The brushy tangle crackled behind me and a grunt from deep within some burly antlered thing "uur-ped" out. Night coming means pulse quickening when lives are at stake. How will my fortune define another's fate? Bucks wander in search of woo. I am watching and wanting too. Woodcock spiraling, whitetails wandering, solace growing. My grip on the death deliverer loosened. My heart listened to the moonlit music. In the quest called hunting there is more to gather than venison. Cold descended with the woodcocks' rising. My soul simmered in the moment's melding. There is no expectation beyond what leftover light illumes. It is timberdoodle time.

MURMURATION

a wave of dark birds
surges
a black feathered river
rustles
flows on eventide
undulates tree-line to horizon
soot-washed
smudged on day-failing sky
does full moon's waning
pull restless flock to roost?
shortening time fails its own patience
to offer response
as heart's glow pulses brighter in bittering cold

SPARROW ENVY

Were I the sparrow
brown-backed skittish and small—
I would find haven
in thorniest thickets—
search far and wide for fields lain fallow
treasure the unkempt
worship the unmown
covet the weed-strewn row

I would slink
between sedges
chip unseen from brambles
skulk deep within hedges
and desire the ditches grown wild

I would find great joy
in the mist-sodden morning
sing humble pleas
from the highest weeds
and plead
for the gray days to stay

FIELD MARK 8: NECESSARY GREED

Gluttony. All along it was gluttony. The shadow bird, the olive-backed spiral song slinger; the Swainson's thrush skulking haint-like in my sideyard thicket for the past few days—was likely drawn down from northbound migratory flight to rest, and to secure food. Fuel for the journey and ground time to reset. This in itself, was not news. It is what migratory birds do. But how did it know there was a bounty waiting in my Piedmont neighborhood? Was there some signal—an aroma wafting in the air? A glimpse of fruit from on high? A memory from last year? Some mysteriously mystically evolved avian super sense? Was there some voice that said—"Stop here"?

I'll never know ultimate bird motivation, and so I'll continue to guess. The reason for my buffy-cheeked guest's lingering, I suspect, is the limbs hanging heavy with purple blackberries.

Just as the waxwings, robins, red-bellied woodpeckers, summer tanagers, and squirrels discovered, it was drawn in, or at least bribed to stay, by berries. And so as it sang this evening, threw that wheezy hornpipe of a song skyward, I wondered if it was a pre-flight *zugunruhe*-driven plan. And then watching it dart furtively from dark thicket into failing light to pluck a quick bite—I realized that hyperphagy might be the motivator in the moment. Greed feeds need. That's my thumbnail hypothesis as I wonder how much longer it will remain. If indeed my assumption is valid of this bird today being the same as the one earlier observed.

In any case, I'm happiest here today, on this bit of fragmented, non-native plant overrun, feral-cat-filled, over-developed land. Happy that my postage stamp piece of Anthropocene-inflamed earth provides some relief; some sustenance for the longer journey to come. A fruit-filled, fattening, fighting chance for a barely-seen bird I've come to almost love.

OCTOROON WARBLER

As a taxonomic committee of one,
I alone have decided
that the past transgressions of long ago dead and rotted
bird watchers must be amended.
That it is my sole responsibility—and pleasure—
to right the wrongs
of racist slave-holding artist ornithologists.
of genocidal complicit naturalists.
of grave-robbing skull-fondling phrenologists.
of the lot of white-supremacist men with the
self-serving penchant
for naming things after themselves.
I hereby declare my solo vote singularly unanimous.
Everything I decide here and now—
passes.
So shall it be written. Let it be done.
Word is bond.
My opinions good as any other treaty
signed in the shifting sand of time.
I do hereby exchange, alter or replace
the names of the birds that follow.
Their former identities by patriarchal rule to be expunged.
That they should have new identities
by my demand.

Bachman's sparrow, denizen of long-leaf pine savannah;
of wiregrass, of fire-kissed sandy ground
shall be once again be
"pine woods."
A true great again recovery worthy of celebration!

And whilst I'm releasing species from bondage,
consider the likely forever gone warbler
of the same Charleston preacher's
human-chattel-possessing label,
can we not do better?
Yes.
"Swamp Cane warbler,"
appropriately by design of damp dank place
it so chose when still in existence, escaping notice.
I would have suggested "Tubman's warbler,"
but then why make it any easier to erase blackness
when extinction has already done the job?
LeConte's Sparrow will hence forward be
"orange-faced."
The brown-backed secretive skulker
of wet weedy rank with tangled overgrown fields,
hider in thickety traces, deserves better fate than linkage
to a Confederate armorer working
to put in place a permanent apartheid nation.

Townsend's Solitaire,
thrush-esque thing of western slope migration
is now "Up-and-Down Solitaire."
Mobile altitudinal propensity
taken into full account.

The lemon yellow-headed black and white
western jewel of a warbler
tagged by that same Indian grave-robbing man,
shall now be a "Doug Fir" specifically,
known for its tie to evergreen boughs.
No disarticulated Native heads required.

To correct an oversight
of Manifest Destiny,
(and opening the western door to indigenous genocide
not accepted),
behold Clarke's Nutcracker,
the capacious resourceful intelligent corvid,
given title by the fire-haired Captain of the Corps!
Henceforth shall be York's Crow.
Designated the first bird so named for a man of color
About damn time the brother got credit
for saving the Corps of Discovery's always imperiled bacon.
Even as property his contributions went largely
without merit.

To even the score a bit more
redact the other leader Lewis
from the northern Rockies woodpecker.
He of Trail of Tears Cherokee removal infamy.
Christen the gorgeous picid Sacagawea's Woodpecker
instead.

As for John James Audubon,
"JJ," if I might?
He of the posed painted birds,
of ego larger than life to go along
with his Baby Elephant folio.
What does a slave-owning,
man-passing for white might deserve?
What might the demigod of birdome merit
after all these years?

Let his name now be struck.
For malfeasance to humanity.
For being prickish and a generally abhorrent man,
Audubon's orioles shall be Rio Grande.
The sea-going petrel with the artist's moniker shall now be
"Warm-Sea Wanderer."
An identity worthy of its tropic-trotting status.

And last but not least, for review
the yellow-rumped warbler of occidental "race,"
occurring beyond the Mississippi to points beyond that.
Since Johnny couldn't bear the very thought
of interracial miscegenation,
let's call the butter-butted bird what it is
in hindsight of his own mixed-raced denial.
The Octoroon Warbler.

Thus, I proclaim on this very day,
whenever this ruling shall be read on whatever future date,
that we remember the identity of the birds for what they are,
and never forget the sins of past imperfections too,
to not repeat the hubris of taking good for granted.
But letting creatures have their own names.
No interference from haters required.

NO MURDER OF CROWS

I watched a flock of crows
fly by,
counted forty-two black souls, then up to sixty-five,
maybe more.
Not sure whether fish or 'merican
They were silent as coal,
headed to roost I assumed,
a congregation I refused to call a murder
because profiling ain't what I do:
besides,
they was just flyin' by.
No cause to criminalize the corvid kind.

THRUSH LUST

A thrush
would rather
you have it
in   pieces.
Eye
for
purple berry.
Tawny throat dawn's first
hidden shadow.
Moss olive brown back blending
fawn spotted breast
into
dappled evening light
tumbled
through September's
      fatigue green
failing.
It is a jigsaw puzzled thing
until a ripening want calls,

                    —hangs—

Tempts.
Hidden form revealed cannot resist
what begs taking.
Is whole until
the mystery thinks better
of what it knows itself
to be.

A secret whisper on night wind
fades quiet into imagining.
Fragments
scattered. to. past. tense.
A hushed wish,
un-
believed.

MIGRATION

what thoughts ramble
in the redstart's brain
as the day draws closed
as dusk descends?
is it larval fuel to lay on fat?
a steady southbound wind?
perhaps it's the flicker
of unseen light
the lure of tropical terrain
is it the flight plan hard-wired—
instinct etched in
by design not likely to change?
or does some warbler learned plan B
come into play
by circumstance rearrange?
fare thee well little bird
may stars bright guide you true
to thicket lush
past falcon's rush
through dark skies inky blue
it's my hope
that neither cat
nor glass
will spell your odyssey's end

but that your tiny wings
some luck
some skill
will bring you back
to inspire me
once again

ICTERID INDECISION

A give and take
between field and forest.
An ebb of grackles; a flow of blackbirds
hordes of blackness,
back and forth from tree-naked crown
to bare ground.
A tide of feathers high
then low.
A flood loosed over weeds died to brown,
covering crops gone to seed.
Sunflower heads bowed to their yellow God
hidden for the day behind clouds.
Then—
as if a single soul among the tens of thousands
(I never counted)
found inspiration
imagined itself the lone wheel;
the pivot in a swirling, sweeping design
of legions in unison flying—
gave by rusty hinged call
(or some icterid whispered sign
only understood by the black-plumaged kind)
the command.
But lacking conviction,
as many but not all flew in gathered mass,

A sphere half-pulsing,

rushed to rising,

a single shushing of millions of feathers pinioning

one against another,

and the other multiplied over and over

and over.

Swushing again to swishing

then a single turn

as if to grow to something greater.

Collapsed to quiet.

Just a murmur.

Silence—

save the conversation

over consumption.

All in the uprising settled back to indecision.

The tide recedes.

Forest to field

then back again.

A DREAM OF SWANS

I saw their pale feathered forms flying through the glow of a waxing moon. I could feel their wild hearts' murmurings; I longed as they did for other places far away but close to heart. I took flight in that swan dream. I took flight and sailed with kindred spirits over salt marsh and fallow field. The earth— landscapes sprawled in space and flattened in time—passed beneath the folding and unfolding of my wings. I was of it all and yet not a part of any that was. I murmured too. I murmured a sweet and sad swan song whispering in the way that wild winged things do of wanderings and wanting and wishing for the felt—but unseen. In my dream flight my wings whooshed and my voice was no longer my own and my swan soul moaned and the peeping frogs peeped from their ponds and the tide rose and fell on the ocean's swell because desire deemed it so. In that swan dream as I flew across the waxing bay moon my breast ached with strokes urgent rowed against imagined sky and yet when I woke—I found that I did not fly.

NOCTURNE

Overhead

   I heard the night songs
of thrushes
        the trills
the thrips and wurps
 of brown backed birds
        with hopes hitched to stars,
flying on faith of light in the dark.
                       Unseen—
but for the sound of them above
        cleaving ink black sky,

millions of souls riding the wind
to some other world.

I thought them at first dreams
    but for the words they left
in echoes of their wings.

DUCK HAWK

for J.A. Baker

Almost faster than I could see
or follow through the clear air
with bare human eyes,
a peregrine streaked.
Beyond flying,
it was projectile
more than feathered thing.
It circled and swooped in figure eights—
a blur hurtling earthward
stooping in a wing-folded dive.
Then suddenly skyward in an arcing
climb over the line it just traced,
ignoring gravity
in the sinuous movement up
defying the pull to ground,
it rose
then dove again
and then once more ascended
on infinite repeating line.
All the while its wings never moved more than to compress
and make it a taloned dart
or opened swept back as check-sail
steering it into perfect turn.
The work looked easy
the bird rode the wind,
never flapping.

I watched with tearing eyes unbelieving—unblinking.
The falcon screamed.
I felt the wild deep within
and counted it
like the perfect curves
carved above the valley floor
sine of infinite hope
a fear of living to overcome.

WREN R. E. M.

fleeting dreams
pass on morning's first light
mist lifting off a mental bridge to nowhere probable—
but all points beyond possible
reality is the wren that wakes to each sun's rising
with only the moment before it
no plans to skulk
or explore the next darkest crevice or crack
it sings heart-full to the limits of the bounds it knows—
the rotting woodpile in the northeast corner
the honeysuckle tangle westward
satisfied in that half acre universe
it sings to meet the day
tucks its wings satisfied in some second of accomplishment
it scolds a plan
and flits away
a wanderer in the present tense
future perfect does not exist
the past makes little sense
that I should live as wisely as wrens
is lesson one
carpe diem ad infinitum

EGG BLUES

Nature versus nurture.
Or so the dichotomy allegedly goes.
The hard-wired instinct of our base being—
blamed on genes.
While the learning and exposure
of our surroundings casts shadows
on our gnarled and twisted family trees.
Who takes care of whom?
Knows the itches to scratch?
Can find the place where you retreat
within your own wildness to escape—
but leave you there trusting you'll return?
The right or wrong questions to ask?
It's all a matter of timing—
the who and what of our *when*-ness.
The birds find their own answers to these questions.
Simply living by codes we can't quite figure out
except to guess, really.
I'm okay with not knowing it all, these days.
Five cerulean eggs lain warm in a cup fashioned
of pine straw and rootlets wound just so
are proof of my human built conceit.
Who taught them this?
The old box hung tenuously on a fence post with no roof.
Dangerously exposed.

Evidence of some bluebird genius faith
unmeasurable by us?—Or is it some sign of persistence?
Maybe an ill-fated nesting move?
The choice has been made beyond my ego grade.
And so for today I'll just take it as a sign
of Sialia sialis love.
I move on to watch a sparrow throw its head back,
and sling its buzzy song into the morning wind
All of the questions I never answered just moments ago
have just begun again.

HOME FROM GUATEMALA (NO WALLS HERE)

the neighborhood wood thrush somehow
found its way back through tempests
past talons
over sea and stopover that used to be
it found the struggling woodlot
—home again—
a few acres of oaks and tulip poplars loblolly pines
everywhere
dogwood and redbuds scatter-blooming underneath
all of it suffocating slowly in kudzu choking on
privet
swarmed over with hungry neglected tabby cats
cowbirds waiting
for evolutionary welfare this evening
though
I forgot all the imperfections when the wood
thrush returned and the notes drifted
through me
it slung its song straight into my heart the harmony
it made with itself
hung onto heaven pierced my
soul brought back love
from a place I'd never known

LESSER
BEASTS

WEED WORSHIP

summer senesces
salidago glows
bidens explodes
glimmering sunlight
gilds saffron shadows

beauty
overruns rank ditches
spills down ragged shoulders
graces forgotten lanes

warmth seeps down
slanting
cutting hours shortening days

wallowing in my own equinox
change creeps inward
pulls heartward
shifts desire to overdrive
before will withers

FIELD MARK 52: GESTALT

A warmer winter day—I revisited the scalped clearcut that's presently wearing a scraggly scruff of scrubby weeds and stumps. I wandered noisily through the tangles, stepping up on the amputated remains of a slain sylvan giant every now and again to get the lay of things and to see who else might be wandering. Bluebirds seem to relish the new open floor plan. They gather in flocks this time of year flashing shades of cobalt against an otherwise bleak canvas of what was. Odd how trees hide hills and holes that only become evident once they're gone.

I made it down to the farthest edge of the bare block today and found hope where the foresters wisely left the hardwood buffer alongside the river. After the satisfying act of tearing apart a poacher's stand, I found an old metal ladder perch that I'd put in the little bottom some five or six years ago, hoping to try and outsmart the old antlered king I'd seen signs of in the privet hell. Finding my stand in the harvest aftermath was like finding a piece of home after a storm has tossed everything else asunder. I climbed up, watched a sharp-shinned hawk recycle some unfortunate songbird and listened to the lucky trees that were left talking in leaf rattle to the river rushing by.

The land laid bare behind me was the same place where the pretty ten-point buck came in to my calling almost a year ago.

He was nose-to-ground in doe seeking mode. I stumbled upon him, wandering on the far edge of the eighty or so acres that had been liquidated. A favorable wind and a glint of antler in late morning sunlight gave him away. A few grunts and bleats later—careful aim through the hyperventilation and the concentrated contraction of my index finger against the spring-taught metal sickle reduced curiosity to fatal flaw.

The nearly sixty pounds of venison the buck sacrificed are nearly gone now, but my memories of him, the hunt and how this place once thick with forest—but now denuded except for stumps, sneeze weed, and sweetgum sprouts—haunts me. Yes, the forest will regrow, and yes—the stunted pines, winged elm and tangles of sweetgum needed a new start for the landowner to gain enough financial ground to hold on to the land. But because hundred-year-old beeches, thick-trunked maples, and understory consorts of dogwood and ironwood got taken to the chip mill too, I was saddened.

Sitting high today in what remains lessens some of the loss. Proof I suppose that there's redemption to be gained even in the bleakest of circumstances.

LIFELESS LIST

Do you know
how hard it is
to admire plumage on a bird?
To separate one warbler chip note
from another?
Or count
the telltale hind wing spots
on a butterfly?
Or remember the name of a wildflower
seen a hundred times?
Or gather the energy to find the
Latin binomial of a beetle in a field guide?
Or even give a fuck what the name
of anything is
beyond the last Black body that
lay still after being murdered
by the police?
I can no longer keep track
of the last hurricane that blew in from the earth's rising heat.
Of the last tweet inciting riot.
The last fire that burned and burned
and burned.
Of the hundreds of thousands of infected and dead.
It is a sad exhausting lifeless list I'd rather not keep,
growing longer by the hour.

There's little room left in my heart these dark days
for listing anything.
Hardest task comes
in not becoming a member
of a litany of dread.

FIELD MARK 2: AWEGASM (N.)

The quasi-erotic, para-sensual overwhelm of the senses, especially in response to nature and non-human beings or the associated phenomena of wildness such as the flight of an otherworldly bird (e.g. swallow-tailed kite), a heart-rending saltmarsh sunset bleeding through dusk, a Blue Ridge mountain sunrise peeling through holler rising fog, or a waxing gibbous moon interrupted by tundra swan flight. It may result in the oozing of unintelligible words of joy and bliss with the spurt-eruption of expletives at eco-climax. Tears and uncontrolled laughter may occur simultaneously. *See also dewkist, feralize, fern-fondling (fiddleheading), lunar lust, treehug, wanton-wander.*

\ *LUV* \

Love,
is the feathered thing
tundra swan flying
across full moon's cold light
wood thrush
singing deep
in redbud blushing spring
wing of wandering owl
sweeping arctic white

Love,
is the wild place
windswept shore
where tide tosses time
cypress swamps ink wet reflection
old field languishing
broom-sedge burnishing gold
in autumn setting sun

Love,
is humid summer
lust crush
cicada's humming choir
leaf's first blush—
verdance
to vermilion warblers wandering
by guiding star

FIELD MARK 25: DUM SPIRO SPERO

In these up and down days of fear. Of exhausting stress. Of breaking strain. Of questions unanswered. Of discord. Any comfort reliably, infallibly yet comes in the sun resting westward and leaving light that stops my heart and makes it beat all the more rapidly at once. It comes in the birds still remaining, hurtling themselves across the face of a waxing moon journeying to places better than here. I envy them in that courage to go where they must: in an obedience to follow wandering's pull. In these things I can rest my waning faith. It is not in any being of rumored omniscience or in four-walled religion beyond earth and sky and day and night—and those beasts and hours that fall in between what we can see or what we might believe.

Until such time as the sun ceases to set in the west or migrating birds no longer ply dark heaven following guiding stars, I hope. I watch. I breathe.

FIELD MARK 6: LOVE HANDLE

Handle any life in your hands as if it were your own. Feel the heart beating—small as it may be—and imagine it in your own chest: beating in syncopated time to become shared meter. That pulse, the breathing, is your rhythm. Your in's and out's: its in's and out's. Look close under whatever warty skin or soft fur or gaudy feathers and see self. Its being is your being. Be in that same skin for what moments it will allow. Then, when the convergence between you is sealed, release that wild soul to free roaming as you would desire of your own.

HARD PAN LIFE

I once watched a mule team, hitched collar to harness to yoke to plow, strain and heave as the blades cleaved apart the hard pan soil as if it were a dirty sea to be sailed through. "Up team!"

"Up Beulah! Les' go Jim!" The order came firm but fell soft on the pair. They knew the work ahead. Looked back at the brown-skinned man briefly to make sure it was the one they could trust. Leaned into the collars and took off.

Every muscle rippled beneath bay and roan coats. The breath of the bay came heavy but even, hot through an open mouth with yellow horse teeth grimaced bare. His jack-assed ears taken from his mammoth Jack dad, lay back against the short-cropped main and thick neck as if to cut the tension hanging thick in the September air. The broad-shouldered roan, the younger Jenny, barely broke a sweat. Her ears shorter by a finger the product of her Percheron mama. She stood a hand or two above the male but knew already how to measure her longer gait to make the twosome one. Head down and eyes straight ahead, her nostrils flared as heart's engine stroked the piston deep within. She and him. Beulah Mae and Jim. They leaned into the work with equal strain. The leather collar creaked as if it would break but never gave way. With hooves gaining purchase—with barely another word from the old

Black man holding the reins. They knew well the terrain and went at the job with nothing but oats, wheat straw, and rest as pay when the lower field was done.

The ground roiled up as they steady went on. Old forged steel sliced into Cecil loam as knife whetstone honed might cut into hot fresh bread. Laid it open so you could see clay deep down coming up red. Yard by yard the team plodded on. Gee'd 'n hawed at the row's end. It seemed they knew the ground better than the old boganned farmer. His forty-three acres sat large. Fields rich with creek flood alluvium. The dirt before the blade become friable soil behind it. Ready to receive seed and rain for the next refrain of winter wheat to sprout up and throw heads when all else green was dead. The roan brayed. The bay followed suit. A barred owl let loose a call from the swamp as the evening dimmed to dusk and fell. Each step closer to the acreage being fully tilled the pair seemed stronger in the harness. "Step up now!" the driver said, harness laid over his own shoulders so he could feel the rest of the way home. They knew the old barn was that much nearer. They leaned in harder still.

Even mules need down time. Beasts of burden are not soulless bags of flesh and bone but feeling beings in need of caring. The plowman knew this. The land they all worked grew crops well but held the legacy of too much bitter before it

ever bloomed sweet. He owned now what bondaged ances-
tors could not. The mules were a promise made to times past.
A promise kept to those never met. The team sweat lathered
and tired. Deserved watering. Earned dinner. Needed rest. An
extra measure of grain was in order. A bath would wash the
sweat away with warm soapy water, curry out the matted hair
to ease the strain, then rub the liniment on to ease fatigue. On
the way in he'd slip Jim a ripe apple from the orchard. Give
Beulah Mae the carrot from his pocket that he'd rooted up
from the garden.

The day closed in on night as the last rows opened up. I heard
the leather creaking, the rigging buckles ringing. Equine
exhaustion smells heavy sweetly musty of horsepower made
step by step. I watched from the road, until I could not see,
imagining myself in the furrow pulling the plow with no help.
The owl called again to remind me of the time.

The yoke I bore was neither oiled leather nor long rein but
being myself with all the expectations from everyone else. The
hardest ground to plow was living fully without worry, not in
the past gone on or future yet to come—but in the present
hardpan now.

SOUND THINKING

the ocean gives
and takes
by time and tide
creates
and destroys with each surge—
lapping away at the edge
of what we know
I'm picking at leftovers—
scavenging
sharing surf with sandpipers and turnstones
plundering plovers
treasuring things the abyss didn't want
the birds find morsels of mussel
and invisible things buried in the sand
I scan the broken bits of aliens
sent asunder by storms
constellations of fallen starfish
moon snails and angel's wings
ripped from reef and wrack
empty houses, the deep dispossessed
lie sea-strewn along the St. Helena strand
a hermit repossesses the foreclosure
scuttles away with the deal
tucks away in security dealt by death
sure in the uncertainty each wave, washes to and fro
sheltered

by some confidence that I don't possess
I saunter along the daily disaster dealt by the deep
hoarding truth into pockets
holding shards of sunlight
in a memory already full
thinking too much about what is
maybe wanting what isn't
lacking a hiding hole
or a shell strong enough to see me through
I exist exposed on some intertidal plain
live naked
in between high water wishes and low tide wants
unbalanced on the shifting of should and should not
a gull hangs in the wind
and laughs at my indecision to just be

ON FINDING SWAMP RELIGION

There is forever here.
Some tree falling down
giving itself up to gravity.
Most do not surrender voluntarily, though.
Entropy comes as the grim reaper to woods.
As wind or flood or hungry bug,
makes dying the only choice,
the trees reclaim rightful place as moss
as mushroom
as litter mold.
Some hang on by tip up mound
a few roots still gripping earth,
the remainder with arms raised heaven high.
Can their rapture be far behind?
Still giving life.
Woodpeckers honor them with much pecking
genuflection and holes.

The Gospel According to Decay.
Everything is wet or dead—or will be soon.

I had a universe to myself.
Alone. No one else in my own image.
Thank you rain. And thank you for late sleepers;
and for others' responsibilities to their four-wall gods.

They have theirs.
I have mine.

My gospel this morning:
Nothing is as it was,
Or will ever be
Again.
Others come to worship.
Peace be done.
Amen.

CHIRICAHUA DREAMING

Across rock-strewn folds, along rifts
sand drifts to mountains
sifts away in sudden rains
red stones burnish to bruised purple hues

from eagle's eyes
a wandering across a cloud-strewn horizon
points the way
to nowhere
out there
and inside—
where the wild hearts beat

a canyon wren calls
tinkles like cool spring water down
my spine

the world's weight
drop it
when forever flies over on a black hawk's shadow

COMPASSING

Limitless is a faraway place
way beyond the hogback ridge named possibility

it's over there
through a tangle-thick forest the old ones call maybe
it is a fortnight's trudge through what could be
and at least as far as a strong man can chunk a stone
—straight as the crow flies
a hard tough row across the mind's breadth
a frog's hair from probable and head high from unreachable
you can't get there from here;
but you can get here from there
it's in the next holler

unfurl the map
aim the compass well
cause true north does lie
dead reckon instead on reality
find yourself there

BUFFALO TRACE

I watched an ant
trek across the landscape
of a bison skull,
antennae wavering
in wonder at the expanse
of great plainness.
It seemed a dry hard place to be,
a desert of dead bone with fissured canyons;
channels.
Dark chasms emptied of cow eyes
that once rolled wild, but void now,
plunging down into an empty cavern
where a bovine brain sat once,
remembering (perhaps)
ancestors uncountable on two-toed feet.
The intrepid hymenopteran traced
the narrow rims of those sockets,
scaled the peak of horn as if it were ant Everest.
Could it be that six legs
makes the wandering any easier?
Do its ant ears catch the echoes of herds past?
Can it sense the thundering rumble
under each little foot? The tumbling of a
band over a cliff to its death?
In and out. Up and down.

The tiny traveler made its way across
the abysmal plain to parts unknown,
packing nothing more than what ants carry
on such expeditions. No cut leaves
or sugar grains on board,
now seemed a heavy enough load
for its half dozen limbs—
or my four.

SOULFUL WARMING

cold creeps in
a gray chill settles
darkness fills
where sunlight fails
cardinal chants
in tangled bramble
towhee kick-scatters leaves
and care
take heart
grasp hope
feathers lighten
solstice's darkening burden
brightening briefest day

FIELD MARK 73: HOW TO JUST BE

Real world means inside obligations to tend to. Widget making. Deadlines pressing. Bills always due. More and more four walls feels like a trap—a cage with no escape. Not being out; not wandering somewhere wild—seems sinful. There's something wonderful I'm not witnessing. Some bird or beast flies or creeps by as I stare into someone else's expectational chasm. It's an expanse I'm increasingly unwilling to span. A new sun warms in brilliant hues. The same tiring orb sinks into the abysmal blue. When that coming and going cycles absent my firsthand witness, I'm squandering time. If wildness is a wish then I'm rubbing the lamp hard for a million more wandering moments.

COVEY OF ONE

Today,
searching for the hidden thing but not sure what.
Questing for hopeful
in open fields among fence lines and under forever horizons.
Birds sing
waiting for responses.
A single quail calls and waits for whistled answer
but none comes.
He is a sad and wishful covey of one
having placed faith in what might never be.
Sparrows throw thin songs into tussocks of rank green grass
and in their wistful pleas I find a bit of what's lost.

I am the tangled fence line gone to weeds in benign neglect.
I am more rusted barbed-wire than gleam and gloss
twisted loose and sagging each day more than taut-straight.
I'd rather bouquets of hawkweed, toadflax, and henbit
than vase-tamed rose any day.

That a meadowlark knows by heart the time
in passing clouds or brightness of sky,
perhaps tosses sweet bubbling notes
in some act of unknowable joy,
teaches me that there is little sense in asking why.

But rather,
that simply perching still in some momentary shadow of now.
I'll sing a thin song too
in my fallow and overgrown thicket where love skulks
and hides within.

GRAVITY (ALWAYS WINS)

summer solstice soul searching
wondering in the shadow of a swollen moon
pondering time and tide
highs and lows
matching ebbs and flows
I wander about in the perigee of my own orbit
elliptically touching self-identity
only to be pulled away
by some unknown sun
slung into the apogeal abyss of space and uncertainty
I gaze skyward into the big orb's glow as it torches trees
in cold light
and yet no fire burns
save those I ignite
I bask in the waxing
bemoan the waning
losing and gaining all the while staying the same
wishing for myself
my being
my own heaven to claim

NON-STATIONARY CYCLING

Year by year we count age in candles and stages. But among the woods and the wetlands, among wild things, life's count does not stop for celebration.

Wandering in the winter woods yesterday, I sensed an urgency underneath the leaf litter. The damp mustiness hanging heavily in the decay ultimately means rebirth. Waiting seeds and warming soil are a promise for another season waged against weather and chance.

A doe's skull found bare and shining ivory, on the white oak ridge meant end and continuance.

I wonder if coyotes make wishes on such things? Did the voided canid skull I found in the fern-full creek bottom mean that the god of wild things had exacted some kind of karma and taken a song dog's life for a deer's? I let lie the evidence to become something else.

Yes, there is something lying in wait in these winter woods—lying and waiting in root and stem and shoot—waiting for the sun to shine more purposefully, for the light to linger a little longer with each day's passage. The wild ginger blooms modestly where no one can see. A wren sang somewhere in a shaft of sun that fractured the chill.

In the depths of what we call the dormant season, frogs a-peeping in secret pools and maples a-blushing against a bare-boned forest are sign certain that life will out and impatiently so—again and again.

BACK ROAD

day failing sun
burns evening blue
to twilight purple hue
then ignites pine-studded tree line
to saffron suddenness
each somber green needle candles into torch
each dying ray scorches memory

—deep

night stalks back road boundaries
time chases hope
and the light leaves in murmurs
sprinkled across stubble-strewn cornfield—
where the last lark song
lingers
and then settles on the fading edges
between seeing
and believing

FIELD MARK 5: HOW NOT TO WATCH BIRDS

Going out this morning to sit in my pickup truck on the side of the road to watch birds. To escape for a few hours in other breathing beings' lives. To envy who they are. To revel for just an hour or two in their songs. But then, I hesitate, wondering what's happened overnight? What city burns? Who's alive? Who's dead? Can a blue grosbeak change human plight? Can an eastern meadowlark's territorial claim to sunrise, orange sky, or the right to breathe without death in the offing, become for a moment my own dream? Just thinking there might be some way to be where I am in my Black skin and not wonder if I'm being trailed, tailed, watched, surveilled, sized up to be brought down? Still thinking on it—whether I should go to some wide open field with clouds and grass; sit among grasshopper sparrows balanced on thin wires concerned with nothing else but being themselves. Lucky birds. Troubled man.

BOHICKET ROAD RAMBLE: FLASH FRY GENTRIFY

Slidin' down Bohicket—
skinny black snake ribbon of two lane
all greased up n' snot slick with spittin' drizzle
tryin' hard not to be one of the dead the live oaks claim
don't wanna give my name to one of those roadside graves
epitaph scribbled skid-mark quick in asphalt
when the swerve came on too quick
a straight stretch can fool you when it suddenly ain't
an unseen curve bent on killin'
memories lie deep in the oak wood's tight-packed grain
three-hundred-year-old souls don't budge for Mercedes
not even an S-Class or a Bimmer Z
those trees
—damn things—
gnarled and stubborn like crotchety old men—
given only to respecting the odd hurricane or two.
those old Bohicket souls
—beenyas—
done watched wildness come and go
seen skeeter-fested swamp change from Black hands to white
Gullah slave land to swamp worth not a red cent

That mucky hell came up for cheap sale
carpetbaggers moved down
made miserable marsh paradise
hunted duck

rode horses behind hounds chasing deer
got busy killin'
grew richer by the year
worthless sells for millions
dark folks that worked the land can't even pay rent
them ol' Bohicket souls done seen it all
but the finest German engineering don't mean shit
when you big around as a house
steel and glass just turn to trash
when high end Euro speed meets old growth oak intent

Scraggly moss beards hang from every tree
southern comfort is what they'd seem to be
fluttering like flags in the sulphur funk of pluff mud
layin' on the breeze

Ain't much genteel about wood hard as concrete
that white cross tacked on the side oughta be ample sign
glimpses of haints roamin' the pitch dark road on foggy nights
say slow down a bit
hug that yellow line
but then—
there's always that one short on patience—
silver Lexus sedan riding my pickup's ample ass
intent on pushing the legal limit
pressing me to do the same

Sixty-thousand-dollar cars ain't gon' wait
there's better living ahead

The brunette chick in the rear view flew down I-95
Michelin rubber on fire
all Manhattean brown stone, tax-bracketed one percent
smug as a motherfucker behind polarized privilege
sped down here to leave the cold
found herself delayed
trailing my middle-class-dead-deer-hauling ride
my South Cacka pace is way too slow
high beams winka-wink for me to get the truck in high gear
Seabrook and Kiawah are waitin' at land's end
there's a double gin and tonic somewhere near
in the third home with the grass clipped just so
and the whitetails that used to be harried
walking about like dogs prancing for show
'cause behind the guarded gates
camo and rifles ain't likely to be found
no—the residential meat is more properly procured
organic-grass-fed-free-range-humanely-slaughtered cow
bought bloodless

kindly dead
delivered by the pound—
unblinking plastic wrapped and Jenn Air-grill bound

wildness Bohicket's end done been tamed
owner associations' dues assessed and paid
wild must be approved-prescribed
and the weeds only grow where the ordinances allow

All's not lost though
there are still a few beasts to fear I've been told
monster golf course gators
beware that ten-footer on the ninth hole
that mofo is almost as long as an Audi Quattro Drive
If it's in the pond then it's clearly out of play
between you and me we'll let bigass sleeping crocodilians lie

Beyond the McMansioned mentality
on the other side of my small-minded rant
across the brackish creek
where the sweetgrass dances and sways
the Atlantic's surf is surging
the tide is moving in
somewhere
there's an old shallow drafted johnboat a-hangin'
somebody's ready to drop a chicken neck in the hole—
hook a blue crab on the line
float a cast net out
bring dinner in
maybe an ol' boy will be wading in the muck

shotgun in hand—Low Country at heart
huntin' for a mess of marsh hen
to cook up freshly plucked
with giblet gravy and sticky rice
all crispy golden and hot lard fried

Next time I'm slidin' down Bohicket
I'll take careful note
let my piedmont pulse relax—
inhale deep
drop my heart beat to lizard belly low
ignore the pressures pushing ever faster for me to go
I'll ease off the gas—scoot down
sit down
remember the wild me—
the one I truly know
I'll heed the old oaks warnings—
Hey Bo—
Slow ya' roll

FIELD MARK 1: LOVE FOR A SONG

Love is barter—bits of affection traded for pieces of adoration.

Love is desire doled out on the whippoorwill's summer wanting. It is our craving for the meadowlark's ringing song—our longing for spring's greening from our sun-starved spirits down to our bare-toed roots. We seek the winding path and wander until we find the sweet spots—blackwater cypress swamp, tallgrass prairie sweep—the place where moonlight glancing off of tide-slicked stones makes us weep.

We want the wild soul, and a shadow-dwelling wood thrush heaps it on us in self-harmonizing sonata. We revel in wildflower bloom—marvel in the migratory sojourns of birds dodging falling stars. Sink yourself deep in the dizzying dance of pollen-drunk bees. Find hope in the re-leaved canopies of the tallest trees. Wind and water—storm and surf—they can move us to other ends. Therein is the turn on. It's the honey sweet seduction. Nature asks only that we notice—a sunrise here, a sunset there. The surge, that overwhelming inexplicable thing in a swallow's joyous flight or the dawning of new light that melds heart and head into sensual soul in that moment of truly seeing—that is love.

ON CONSIDERING THE HOLOCENE
WITH WHITE MEN

A pile of feathers,
barred tan and brown
dirty and dust-covered
huddled in the shadows of former infrastructure.
Graffiti paintings of
Abe Lincoln maybe smoking a blunt
depict a stark honesty of in between land gone
past marsh muck wet
to throat-sore desiccated dry beyond life.
The owl formerly great
and now limp horned sits in the simmering cool
of a heated day.
Dull yellow eyes blink slow caution
no one pays attention to.
There is no *Bubo virginanus* glare, only listless
half dead owl stare.
Why here? Why now?
Why so tame oh great fierce predator of the night?
We cannot surmise reason or
rationale for what we see.
Only guesses, in feints and jabs
offering half-hearted scientific guesses,
hypotheses of poison or predators
or just the probability of unlucky youth.
Holocene writers on the cusp of imagined Anthropocene
apocalypse make speculation artfully.

Life will not likely persist through the late train
that zooms passengers between this interim lying here
in Yolo hinterland
and somewhere else they will not notice
because their heads are down in their phones.
Skulls of rodents killed,
ripped head from tiny pawed limb
digested,
and coughed up again in neatly packed pellets of bone and fur
reflect the natural history of the hard pan
hard scrabble edge of everything—
expanding urban at the edge of disappearing rural,
super-highway stretching eight lanes wide
beside gravel two track,
risen trestle erected to hyper speed train
and slow pace of four wanderers feeling their way.
Owl blinks.
We leave wondering
Depressed
Knowing
Owl will soon join the other dead things
mapping the coming days.

FIELD MARK 17: GOOD ENOUGH

On many days in my own backyard, I wonder about the birds that somehow find "home" in the postage stamp of waning suburbia that used to be oak, hickory, and pine—but turned by someone's idea of "progress" some forty years ago from wild forest to feral fragment, it's where hosta and privet and mulberry and sunflower and dooryard violet and butterfly bush and struggling tomato reign. In the midst of all that some would claim should not be where "natives" should, I sit and watch and wonder how the wrens, cardinals, robins, chickadees, thrashers, pine warblers, chipping sparrows, house finches, titmice, bluebirds, woodpeckers, doves, mockingbirds, and nuthatches survive. Beyond the glimpses at feeders and fountains and the familiar calls that fall between the audible cracks left by lawn mowers, barking dogs, and passing cars, they seem to make do in a world of "alien invaders." And then my wondering wanders far far away when some exotic visitor from some place far south of my neighborhood knowing decides that this place—my home—is good enough even in its non-native besieged state. There's a call I recognize and high above the weeds I claim as wildflowers, a tropical bird—a great crested flycatcher—finds the box I erected from the remains of a storm-tossed pine a few years back, hoping the real estate would find favor among hole-nesting flycatcher kind. I planted some more zinnias next to the canna lilies. Neither are "native" but who among us truly is. All of us, by free will or force have come here from someplace else. Here—today it seems, the place I call home, is good enough for birds and me too.

FIELD MARK 3: IN REMEMBRANCE (AUTO OBIT)

At the end—to be loved and loving. That will be grand. Children chattering and grown to good. Woodlands walked and wandered. Surf sauntered through. Trees scaled to spy on the waking wood. Streaking stars hauling wishes through an ink black sky. A lingering embrace. That cold night in the desert when first I heard the coyote cry.

DEER WORSHIP

My deer stand is a tower of self-diagnosis. A tall temple of introspection where I see more clearly in the graying dark of lingering night than in desk-bound fluorescence. I climb a pine and leave responsibility behind and expectation on the ground to look out into a realm of wildness that is more mirror than any hanging on walls. There are no promises to break or contracts to breach except those bargained alone to be fully in whatever moment comes. I can clearly see the red-tail hawk rising on unseen hope.

A gray fox finds fall's fortune under a persimmon tree—but I know the sweeter luck lies with me.

The rut-blind buck with nose to ground and white tail wagging to the sky focuses intentions on willing does and making more of his kind. Whether I watch in envy of his freedom or lay cross-hairs heart-lung-high is never simple math. There's free-will and ultimate choice. It is Paradise, Heaven, Nirvana, and Brigadoon with a bit of Rabbit Hole thrown in. All I witness is worthy of worship. Wild things are not burdened with guilt or sin.

It is prayer and meditation and godless pleas thrown as alms and ash into the autumn wind—it is a counseling couch with no limits on listening. Sparrows offer free advice on seed searching. My deer stand is downward facing dog and genuflection—a supplicating place where time is the rare commodity sought and patience the only cost. I watch sun and moon rise circle and rest without rewinds or resets. In my tree commandments don't come in ten, but one—just be.

FIELD MARK 11: SUNSET CAMP

Last night, as whippoorwills called in the holler and frogs made love in shallow pools and katydids and crickets bowed dry wings on dry wings from green leaves in darkening symphony and lightnin' bugs signaled semaphore intent to make more of themselves and twigs snap-crackled beneath the knife-edged hooves of deer—or berry-fatted paws of black bear in the dimmed forest—and the bats flutter-flapped overhead, the three of us calling ourselves poets sat far apart from one another but near enough to the earth to share in the life that emerged from beyond the reach of a world unraveling at the seams of murder and injustice. There is a privilege in this occasional escape and off-grid ignorance that I admit to—that I question the fairness of. I worry as Black men die in the streets, though, I'm too far away to feel the necessary pain. Too high on friends and verse and a beer or two. Not to worry, it all floods in on the drive back when I see the first police car cruising and wonder. Will I make it home?

MEANINGS
&
REGULATORY
RAMBLE

NINE RULES FOR THE BLACK BIRDER

1) Be prepared to be confused with the other black birder. Yes, there are only two of you at the bird festival. Yes, you're wearing a name tag and are six inches taller than he is. Yes, you will be called by his name at least half a dozen times by supposedly observant people who can distinguish gull molts in a blizzard.

2) Carry your binoculars—and three forms of identification—at all times. You'll need the binoculars to pick that tufted duck out of the flock of scaup and ring-necks. You'll need the photo IDs to convince the cops, FBI, Homeland Security, and the flashlight-toting security guard that you're not a terrorist or escaped convict.

3) Don't bird in a hoodie. Ever.

4) Nocturnal birding is a no-no. Yeah, so you're chasing that once-in-a-lifetime rare owl from Outer Mongolia that's blowing up your twitter alert. You're a Black man sneaking around in the nether regions of a suburban park—at dusk, with a spotting scope. Guess what? You're going to have some prolonged conversations with the authorities. Even if you look like Forest Whitaker—especially if you look like Forest Whitaker.

5) Black birds—any black birds—are your birds. The often-overlooked blackbirds, family *Icteridae*, are declining across the board. Then there are the other birds that just happen to be black—crows and their kin are among the smartest things with feathers and wings. They're largely ignored because of their ubiquity and often persecuted because of stereotype and mis-understanding. Sounds like profiling to me.

6) The official word for an African American in cryptic cloth-ing—camo or otherwise—is incognegro. You are a rare bird, easy to see but invisible just the same. Until you snap off the identification of some confusing fall warbler by chip note as it flies overhead at midnight, or a juvie molting shorebird in heavy fog, you will just be a token.

7) Want to see the jaws of blue-blooded birders drop faster than a northern gannet into a shoal of shad? Tell them John James Audubon, the patron saint of American ornithology, had some black blood coursing through his veins. Old JJ's mom was likely part Haitian. Hey, if we can claim Tiger Woods . . .

8) Use what's left of your black-president momentum on the largely liberal birder crowd to step to the front of the spot-ting-scope line to view that wayward smew that wandered into US waters from Eurasia. Tell them you're down with Barack, and they'll move even more to the left to let you look at the doomed duck. After all, you stand about as much of a chance of seeing a smew again as you do of seeing another black president.

9) You're an endangered species—extinction looms. You know all the black birders like siblings and can count them on two hands. You're afraid to have lunch with them all because a single catastrophe could wipe the species from the face of the earth. There's talk and posturing about diversifying the hobby, but the money is not where the mouths are. People buy binoculars that would fund the economy of a small Caribbean island—where, coincidentally, lots of neotropical migratory birds winter, and where local people of color might contribute to their conservation if more birders cared about more than counting birds.

HOW TO ADORE BIRDS

1) Love and appreciate all things with feathers.

2) Everyone has a bird story. EVERYONE.

3) Never ever forget the beauty in the common thing. Take time to recognize the subtle differences in cardinal crest perkiness or crow blackness.

4) Slow down. Absorb birds.

5) Every bird is a life bird. Every time. The first time or the thousandth time. If you're breathing when you see the bird, it's a lifer.

6) Don't take yourself so seriously. Birding is an imperfect craft wrought with ego mines. You will make mistakes. The birds know who they are. If you misidentify them, they don't really care.

7) List birds with your heart. You'll not forget them when written in blood with pulse.

8) Keep a life list of people and places. See beyond your binoculars to understand context and culture. This breeds empathy. Empathy breeds care. Care breeds love.

9) Be the bird. See the miracle in each and every one of them. Conservation is the act of caring so intensely for something that you want only the best for its survival and future being. That intense care and love, is called conservation.

10) Find a way to share your love of not just birds—but nature—with others. Even better if the ones shared with don't share your skin color or ethnicity or gender / nongender designation or religion or...

11) Don't be the birder that causes others to say "Now that's why I don't bird." We don't need more birder police keeping track of missed IDs on fall flycatchers and third-year gulls.

12) Don't be afraid to fall in love with a bird. It's perfectly legal in most states—except maybe Mississippi. I'm not asking you to do anything freaky. Just focus on a bird... for a few minutes, an hour or two—maybe those moments become days and weeks and... Next thing you know your life is birdful!

13) HAVE FUN & WATCH WITH A PURPOSE! Take it all in... boulders, butterflies, birds... understand at the end of the day your life list will be filled with much more than birds.

GROUP THINK: NEW NAMES FOR PLURAL BIRDS

A Hemorrhage of cardinals
red-staining the backyard
A Consideration, Council
or Congress of crows;
call them anything but murderers, please.
A Whir of hummingbirds
A Riff (or Mood) of any bird that's blue

A Thicket of sparrows
A Mine of goldfinches
A Skulk of thrashers
A Cuddle of chickadees. (Cute is a definite field mark.)

A Thuggery of jaegars
A Piracy of skuas

A Crucifixion of shrikes

A Mattering of Black birds—
Lives ignored, hated and dissed.
How did darkness become so despised?

A Melody of thrushes
A Palette of painted buntings
An Audacity of wrens—

finding every crevice ever created
and singing loudest about the fact.
A Vomitus of vultures.

A Swarm of flycatchers—
Empidonax "spuh" be damned.
A Tide of shorebirds—
rising more than falling,
wishful thinking on past abundance;
knots, whimbrel, peeps, plovers, curlews
darkening salt marsh skies.

A Privilege of all birds white—
though it's not their fault
for almost always being given the benefit of doubt or being
mostly respected; usually liked.

An Immigration of starlings.
loved to tears in distant murmuration
but deplored to legalized killing on the street.
Deprived of breath without penalty or cause.

A Herd of cowbirds. Given the gift of never parenting.
Evolutionary brilliance.

A Flurry of snowbirds;
juncos my grandma claimed she pitied
and threw them handfuls of grits.

A Wandering of warblers
An Envy of swallow-tailed kites
A Front of waterfowl
—forecasting gray winter days to come.
A Cache of nuthatches
A Wheeze of gnatcatchers
A Throne of kinglets (or court if you please).

A Missing of Carolina parakeets,
too smart for their own good.
An Echo of passenger pigeons
—billions dwindled to none.
A Memory of ivory-bills
        in praise of the Great Lord God
maybe not all gone.

An Inclusion of mixed migratory flocks,
hopefully integrated by choice
and not forced to co-mingle
in whatever gulfs they must cross.

Wondering what they would call themselves?
If there is disagreement over plumage color, wing bar width,
leg hue, call tone or habitat of origin?

How would they name us? Would the tables turn?
Am I a greater Southern Black-backed two-legged thing?

You perhaps a common White-fronted human being?
Someone else named after a passerine of respectable fame
or raptor of murderous infamy?

Here in gratitude of everyone there ever was—
Whatever the name.
A Love of birds. My collective label.

GLOSSARY

Anthropocene

The current depressing age of human-created and hyper-enhanced woe. Nature still reigns supreme though. *See also* Pandemic.

Bird

Worship-worthy, feather-bearing, winged beings, most of which fly. With abilities to sing in harmony with themselves, move by the millions in murmuration as a single entity and traverse hemispheres guided by stars, they are what humans would be if they could. *See also* Icarus.

Birder

Me.

Bohicket

A ten mile two-lane ribbon of asphalt black snake that stretches across John's Island in Charleston, South Carolina. The Angel Oak, a huge kraken of a live oak, lives there. It carries the rich through poor places to live in luxury. Drive carefully or the Bohicket snake will crush you.

Canid

Four-legged things that are related to your pooch.

Chiricahua

Majestically jagged, savagely dragon-toothed Southeast Arizona mountains named for a band of courageous and freedom-loving native people, the Apache Indians. They are famed for the exotic birds they harbor.

Cicada

The bug-eyed bugs that begin an incessant—and either pleasantly numbing or irritating—buzzing in the heat of the summer and do not cease until frost freezes them. They emerge from the ground after years of waiting like aliens to climb into trees—buzz; suck sap; buzz; mate; buzz and die.

Clearcut

A forestry term describing a place where all the trees are cut down at once. Clearcuts can be bad and scars on the landscape when carelessly done, or, when managed with care, rich areas of regeneration for a forest to begin again.

Conservation

The intense desire to save something in abundance, left better for future generations who you will not know. *See also* Love and Care.

Dum Spiro Spero (L.)

"While I breathe, I hope." 1. Motto on the seal of my home state of South Carolina, which is much more admirable than being known for secession to preserve slavery. 2. What I, and most Black people, are thinking when being stopped by the police. *See also* George Floyd.

Ecology

Us and them; every living and non-living thing linked in. Same air, same water, same soil, same earth, same fate.
See also Marvin Gaye, "Mercy Mercy Me (The Ecology)"

Field Mark

A part of something that helps you know what the whole thing is. Cardinal beak thickness versus warbler beak thinness, dazzling feather color, a beautiful flute-ish song, waving a Confederate flag claiming, "Heritage not hate."

Holocene

The ten or twelve millenia (an epoch) just passed between woolly mammoths (Pleistocene) and islands of plastic trash (*see also* Anthropocene). It was the geologic recess between humans being eaten by large beasts and humans exacting revenge now, by "extincting" all the large beasts leftover that didn't get them first.

Icterid

A blackbird but not always a black bird—or even all black. Redwings, rusties, Brewer's, grackles, tri-coloreds, yellow-headed's, orioles, troupials, oropendolas, meadowlarks, cowbirds—but not crows or ravens or starlings. And no, they don't all look alike either.

Lesser Beasts
Anything without feathers or wings. Everything else but those beings called birds. Mostly me.

Murmuration
The mesmerizing wavelike & fluid unified movement of a flock of birds or school of fish. If you say the word to yourself thirteen times you will begin to feel what it means.

Negro (arch.)
Term formerly used by some to describe those of Sub-Saharan Black African heritage. Frequently degraded to "nigra" as the bastard term derived from "nigger." Eventually evolved to colored, black, and presently, African-American or Black. James Baldwin was not yours.

Octaroon (arch.)
An allegedly archaic term mostly used in Louisiana and portions of the Caribbean archipelago to describe a person of questionable color with a drop (or "taint") of Black (negro) blood from a bi-racial grandparent which would render them legally unworthy of humane consideration. *See also* quadroon;

mulatto; half-breed; high yellow; light-skinned; milkman's baby; John James Audubon.

Pandemic

Hell on earth in the form of a "novel" coronavirus likely transmitted between bats and the humans possibly eating them. *See also* COVID-19, also plague.

Racism

The systemic and institutionalized hatred of another person or population because of ethnicity or race. Celebrated as a "Lost Cause" in the United States by bitter losers and conspiracists. Exacted for four centuries on Black folks and even longer against Indigenous and First Nations people. *See also* original sin and cultural denial.

Redstart

A tiny finger-sized sprite belonging to a group of birds called wood warblers. Redstarts are named as such because they are obscenely attired in black and orange (guys) or brown and yellow (gals) and appear as flashes of fire against the new green of spring sprouting trees.

Rutty

The act of being "rutted up;" a sex-crazed season when buck white-tailed deer fight one another, rub trees, piss in the dirt, and seek does so that they can make more of themselves.

Salidago & Bidens (aka goldenrod & tickseed; sun-yellow, wild-flower)
Fall beauties that become prettier with increased negligence and reckless abandon.

Sandpipers & plovers
Smallish, cute & typically brownish beach-dwelling birds that chase waves, skitter-scatter across mudflats, and flash-fly in moments of wanderlust to settle on the next parcel of sand—or another continent.

Senesce
To wither and die over time. Sometimes brilliantly and gloriously, like autumn leaves, but mostly just a drying up and fading to brown to return to soil. Plants do it. So will we.

Sundown Town
Municipalities, towns, villages, or crossroads where by formal declaration or well-heeded rumor, Black people were (are?) to be out of the area before sundown. "Don't let the sun set on you here nigger!" would be the definitive phrase in such a place. Not restricted to the American South. *See also* range map restriction; range limitation; *Green Book*.

Timberdoodle (a.k.a woodcock)
A squat, short-legged, long-beaked, googly-eyed game bird found in places most people would rather not go, such as briary tangles and mirey mucks; sometimes called a bog bat.

Towhee

A large, jaunty sparrow that kicks about in the leaf litter singing "Drink Your Tea!" Where I'm from, they used to be called "rufous-sided towhees," which was a much more accurate and frankly, seductive name until the gene jockeys and name-taggers decided otherwise. Geez. My grandmother called them "Jorees" 'cause that's what their songs sounded like to her.

Wood thrush

A brown-backed, spot-breasted & angelic bird-soul that can throw three self-harmonized notes into the spring air to seduce the unwary wanderer. They are sirens of the forest. I love them.

Wren

Small brown birds with cocked tails and loud songs. They are the Joe Pesci's of the feathered kind, generally loud and unwilling to be ignored. You laughin' at them? Don't.

Zoom

A reality twisting torture chamber of horrors born of viral quarantine (*see also* Pandemic), facilitating virtual engagement from the waist up. Best known phrase "You're on mute."

This "feel guide" to sparrows, thrushes, duck hawks, ants, falling stars, deer, frogs, timberdoodles and lesser human being beasts, is the spawn of an earlier exercise in *Sparrow Envy*, born in the Holocene Press of John Lane. It is an intensification of all that's brown and easily overlooked. Skulky and thicket-loving. —*JDL*

AUTHOR NOTE

DONORS

The Hub City Writers Project thanks our friends who made contributions in support of this book and other Hub City programs.

Patty and C. Mack Amick

Marjorie Boafo and
 Kofi Appiah

Paula and Stan Baker

Valerie and Bill Barnet

Beatrice Bruce

Mary Ann Claud and
 Olin Sansbury

Linda and Bill Cobb

Kirsten and John Cribb

ExxonMobil Foundation

Katherine and
 Charles Frazier

Jeb Gruhntz

Holly and Mike Hoenig

Susu and George Dean
 Johnson

Kim Rostan and
 Matt Johnston

The Rose Montgomery
 Johnston Family
 Foundation

Dorothy and Julian Josey

Margaret Miller

Weston Milliken

Milliken and Co. Charitable
 Foundation

Deborah F. McAbee and
 J. Byron Morris

Carlin and Sander
 Morrison

Dwight Patterson

J.M. Smith Foundation

Betty Snow

Spartanburg County
 Public Libraries

Betsy Teter and John Lane

Jane and Tom Abbott

Betsy Adams

Winthrop Allen

Sarah and Mitch Allen

Ceci and Tom Arthur

Susan C. and Robert D. Atkins

Susan Baker

Georgianna and Harold L. Ballenger

Joan and Tom Barnet

Cyndi and
 David Beacham

Elizabeth D. Bernardin

Bert Barre

Lynne and Mark
  Blackman
Kathryn Boucher
Carol and
  Jim Bradof
Julia Burnett
Kathy and Marvin
  Cann
Harriet Cannon
Camilla and Jeff
  Cantrell
Mary
  Cartledgehayes
Ruth Cate and
  Chuck White
Sally and Randall
  Chambers
Anne and Al
  Chapman
Sally and Jerry
  Cogan, Jr.
Gregory and Molly
  Colbath
Victoria T. Colebank
Rick and Sue
  Conner
William Cooper
Nancy and Paul Cote
Haidee B. and
  Gardner Courson
Tom Moore Craig
Jed Dearybury

Magruder H. Dent
Alice and Chris
  Dorrance
Jean Dunbar
Jane Easler
Alice Eberhardt
Coleman Edmunds
Anne Elliott
Walter Enloe
Carol and Edwin Epps
Angelina Eschauzier
Delie Fort
Abby Fowler
Elaine T. Freeman
Joan Gibson
Sara Goldstein
Elaine and
  Barney Gosnell
Laura and
  John Gramling
Andrew Green
Roger and Marianna
  Habisreutinger
Jo Hackl
Susan Hamilton
Tanya and Benjy Hamm
Anita and Al
  Hammerbeck
Monty Mullen a
  Julian Hankinson
Tracy and Tom
  Hannah

Emily Harbin
Carolyn C. Harbison
Darryl Harmon
Lou Ann and
  John Harrill, Jr.
Michele and
  Peyton Harvey
James Hayes
Laura Beeson
  Henthorn
Patricia Hevener
Coleman Hockett
Charlie Hodge
Marilyn and
  Doug Hubbell
Elsa Hudson
Eliza and Max Hyde
Harriet and David
  Ike
Susan Hodge Irwin
Sadie Jackson
Louise Johnson
Juliet and Thomas
  Johnson
Melissa and Steve
  Johnson
Ann and Stewart
  Johnson
Nancy Tiller & Chip
  Johnson
Rose Johnston
Ann J. Jone

Betsy and Charles
  Jones
Frannie Jordan
Cathryn and Michael
  Judice
Vivian and Daniel
  Kahrs
James Karegeannes
Ann Kelly
Cynthia and Keith
  Kelly
Nancy Kenney
Beverly Knight
John M. Kohler, Jr.
jacque Lancaster
Mary Jane and Cecil
  Lanford
Kay and Jack
  Lawrence
Janice and Wood Lay
Ruth and Joe Lesesne
Francie and Lindsay
  Little
Frances and George
  Loudon
Elizabeth Lowndes
Julie and Brownlee
  Lowry
Cassi MacNaughton
Gayle Magruder

Kari and Phillip
  Mailloux
Nancy Mandlove
Jim Mayo
Wendy Mayrose
Connie McCarley
Judy McCravy
Nan and Tom
  McDaniel
Diana D. McGraw
Ray McManus
Larry E. Milan
Carole and Boyce
  Miller
Deborah Minot
Karen and Bob
  Mitchell
Lynda and Bert Moore
Marsha Moore
Susan Griswold and
  John Morton
Lawrence Moser
Susan Myers
Liz Newall
Margaret and George
  Nixon
Susan and Walter
  Novak
Cecile and Chris
  Nowatka

Hope Nunnery
Mark Olencki
Louise and W. Keith
  Parris
Penni and Steve Patton
Nancy Pemberton
Mary and Andrew
  Poliakoff
Sara and Jan Postma
Mamie Potter
Kay A. and L. Perrin
  Powell
Mary Price
Terry Pruitt
Donna and Norman
  Pulliam
Eileen Rampey
Sharon and Garroll
  Purvis
Ann and Ron Rash
Beverly and Julian
  Reed
Elizabeth Refshauge
Naomi Richardson
Betsy and Ricky
  Richardson
Rose Mary Ritchie
Elisabeth and Regis
  Robe
Renee Romberger

For more information about how to support the Hub City Writers
Project and Hub City Press books, authors, and activities, please visit
www.hubcity.org/support or contact us at info@hubcity.org.

PUBLISHING
New & Extraordinary
VOICES FROM THE
AMERICAN SOUTH

FOUNDED IN Spartanburg, South Carolina in 1995, Hub City Press has emerged as the South's premier independent literary press. Hub City is interested in books with a strong sense of place and is committed to finding and spotlighting extraordinary new and unsung writers from the American South. Our curated list champions diverse authors and books that don't fit into the commercial or academic publishing landscape.

RECENT HUB CITY PRESS POETRY

Cleave • Tiana Nobile

Mustard, Milk, and Gin • Megan Denton Ray

Dusk & Dust • Esteban Rodriguez

Rodeo in Reverse • Lindsey Alexander

Eureka Mill - 20th Anniversary Edition • Ron Rash

Magic City Gospel • Ashley M. Jones

Hub City Press gratefully acknowledges support from the National Endowment for the Arts, the Amazon Literary Partnership, South Arts, and the South Carolina Arts Commission.

Printed in the USA
CPSIA information can be obtained
at www.ICGtesting.com
JSHW020949060424
60304JS00004B/2

9 781938 235818